I'm Thinking of a Little State

Bela Davis

Abdo Kids Junior
is an Imprint of Abdo Kids
abdobooks.com

abdobooks.com

Published by Abdo Kids, a division of ABDO, P.O. Box 398166, Minneapolis, Minnesota 55439.

Printed in the United States of America, North Mankato, Minnesota.

102025

012026

THIS BOOK CONTAINS RECYCLED MATERIALS

Photo Credits: AdobeStock, Getty Images, Shutterstock, ©Corey Templeton p.13/CC BY-NC-ND 2.0, ©Shannon McGee p.23/CC BY-SA 2.0

Production Contributors: Teddy Borth, Jennie Forsberg, Grace Hansen

Design Contributors: Candice Keimig, Pakou Moua

Library of Congress Control Number: 2025936501

Publisher's Cataloging-in-Publication Data

Names: Davis, Bela, author.

Title: I'm thinking of a little state / by Bela Davis

Description: Minneapolis, Minnesota : Abdo Kids, 2026 | Series: I'm thinking of a state | Includes online resources and index.

Identifiers: ISBN 9798384907381 (lib. bdg.) | ISBN 9798384908081 (ebook) | ISBN 9798384908432 (Read-to-Me ebook)

Subjects: LCSH: States, Small--Juvenile literature. | States, Size of--Juvenile literature. | American states (United States)--Juvenile literature. | Geography--Juvenile literature.

Classification: DDC 917--dc23

Table of Contents

Guess the State!

I'm thinking of a little state!

A little state is small in area.

It is under 13,000 square miles (34,000 sq km).

N
W
E
S
Canada
Vermont
New Hampshire
Massachusetts
Rhode Island
Connecticut
New Jersey
Delaware
Maryland
Pacific Ocean
Hawaii
Atlantic Ocean

Can you guess the state?

The state flower is the red clover.

State Clues

- **Flower:** Red clover

The state bird is the hermit **thrush**.

State Clues

- **Flower:** Red clover
- **Bird:** Hermit thrush

Moose live in this state!

State Clues

- **Flower:** Red clover
- **Bird:** Hermit thrush
- **Animal:** Moose

This state has some very fresh maple syrup!

State Clues

- **Flower:** Red clover
- **Bird:** Hermit thrush
- **Animal:** Moose
- **Activity:** Fresh maple syrup

There are many bike trails.

One trail goes across a lake!

State Clues

- **Flower:** Red clover
- **Bird:** Hermit thrush
- **Animal:** Moose
- **Activity:** Fresh maple syrup
- **Visit:** Lake bike trail

15

People explore and camp in Green Mountain **National Forest**.

State Clues

• Flower:	Red clover
• Bird:	Hermit thrush
• Animal:	Moose
• Activity:	Fresh maple syrup
• Visit:	Lake bike trail
• Explore:	Green Mountain

The state's capital is Montpelier.

State Clues

• Flower:	Red clover
• Bird:	Hermit thrush
• Animal:	Moose
• Activity:	Fresh maple syrup
• Visit:	Lake bike trail
• Explore:	Green Mountain
• Capital:	Montpelier

Now you have all the clues! Can you guess what state I'm thinking of?

State Clues

- **Flower:** Red clover
- **Bird:** Hermit thrush
- **Animal:** Moose
- **Activity:** Fresh maple syrup
- **Visit:** Lake bike trail
- **Explore:** Green Mountain
- **Capital:** Montpelier

VT
NH
HI
MA

I'm Thinking of...
Vermont!

Glossary

national forest
a large area of forest that is set aside by the United States government to protect it.

thrush
a common songbird that can be found in many parts of the world. Thrushes are mostly of a plain color often with spotted underparts.

Index